CONTENTS

CHAPTER 1

WHAT IS POP MUSIC?

Have you ever found yourself humming and tapping along to the radio?

At the chorus, did you break suddenly and loudly into song?

Did the tune go around and around in your head for the rest of the day?

That's pop music!

Pop is short for popular music.

All pop songs have the same things in common.

- A "hook" (some words or a tune) that you remen
- Verses and choruses.
- The song is 2.5 to 5.5 minutes long.
- Guitars, bass, drums, keyboards and singing.
- The song is released as a single and bought mainly by young people.
- If enough people buy the song, it will make it onto the music charts.

Music fans listen to the latest pop songs in a 1950s record shop.

The music charts tell us which artist sold the most singles in a week.

Every pop star wants their song to reach "Number 1". They also want it to stay Number 1 for a long time!

Justin Timberlake wins the best pop vocal performance and best pop vocal album at the 2004 Grammy awards.

Success in the charts can make singers and band members rich and famous.

Record companies earn millions of pounds from their top stars.

And the fans?

Millions of pop fans all over the world buy records and dream of meeting their idols!

Jennifer Lopez meets fans at an awards ceremony.

CHAPTER 2
THE EARLY YEARS

Pop music was born in the 1950s. This happened for two reasons. It was when the music charts began, and rock and roll was invented!

Rock and roll was a blend of blues music and country music.

Singers and bands performed the songs. But older, professional songwriters wrote them.

Pop music grew out of 1950s rock and roll.

Elvis played loud, rebellious rock and roll. He also dressed in cool clothes.

Elvis Presley was the world's first pop star.

His singing and dancing outraged parents everywhere.
But teenagers loved him!

Elvis had 18 Number 1 hits. He spent 80 weeks at the top
of the charts. He is one of the most influential artists in
music history.

In the 1960s, young bands began writing their own songs.

In the UK, The Beatles wrote one catchy hit after another.

Their young fans could not buy the records fast enough!

The Beatles had many Number 1 hits in the UK and USA. *Yesterday* is the most covered song in history. It has been recorded over 3,000 times by different artists.

It is thought The Beatles have sold over one billion albums. This makes them the best-selling band of all time.

The Beatles' songs still influence pop artists today.

In the USA, the Motown label was set up to record mainly black artists.

Groups such as The Jackson 5, The Temptations and The Supremes created the "Motown sound". It was a mixture of soul, funk, blues and gospel.

The Supremes had a run of Number 1 hits in the mid 1960s. These included *Baby Love* and *Stop! In the Name of Love*.

The Supremes

CHAPTER 3

THE 1970s

In the 1970s, a new glittering pop scene took over from rock and roll.

In the USA, artists such as Stevie Wonder and Marvin Gaye made sure the Motown sound stayed alive and well in pop music.

In the UK, artists such as David Bowie and Elton John went glam rock! They wore shiny suits and platform boots.

These artists were both singers and songwriters.

David Bowie

Then came disco!

Disco was born from the funk, soul and Latin music played in US nightclubs.

ABBA and the Bee Gees shared the disco throne. They created night fever and dancing queens everywhere!

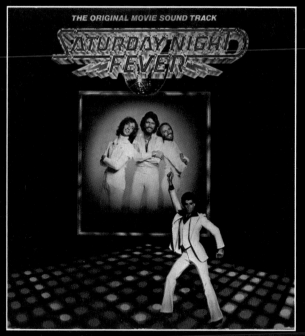

In 1977, the disco movie *Saturday Night Fever* was released. The Bee Gees wrote and performed most of the songs on the soundtrack album.

ABBA

1970s POP PROFILE
ELTON JOHN

- 59 top 40 singles
- Seven Number 1 albums

Elton John's best-selling single is *Candle in the Wind 1997*. It was recorded in 1997 as a tribute to Diana, Princess of Wales. It sold 37 million copies.

> " I always liked spending my money. Even when I was a kid, when I had a paper round. "

Elton John

STEVIE WONDER

- Over 30 top 10 singles
- 12 top 10 albums

Stevie Wonder became blind just hours after he was born. He signed to Motown when he was 11 years old.

 Just because a man lacks the use of his eyes it doesn't mean he lacks vision.

Stevie Wonder

15

CHAPTER 4

THE 1980s

In August 1981, MTV (Music Television) was launched. Now, every new pop single had to have its own music video.

The "look" of a band was as important as their music. Image was everything in the 1980s!

Duran Duran

Duran Duran were one of the "New Romantics" bands. These artists wore frilly shirts, "quiff" hairstyles and eyeliner. They played moody music with good melodies.

Pop songs appeared in TV shows, movies and even in TV ads. Songs were used to sell everything from leg warmers to Rubik's Cubes.

Pop bands started to use new electronic equipment such as synthesizers and drum machines. These machines can produce thousands of different sounds all from a small keyboard device.

Prince became a huge star in the 1980s. He combined R&B, soul, funk, rock, jazz and Hip-Hop to create his own unique pop music.

Prince starred in and wrote the music for the movie Purple Rain.

1980s POP PROFILE
MADONNA

- 150 million singles sold
- 250 million albums sold

Madonna had a single in the top 40 every year from 1983 to 2004 (except for 1988 when she didn't release any singles).

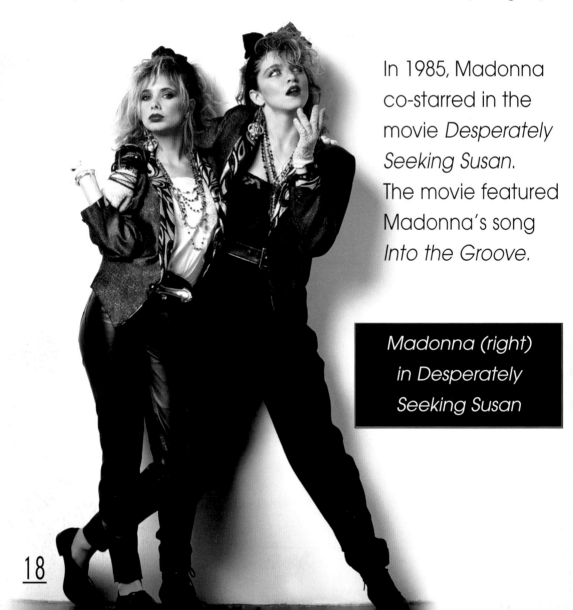

In 1985, Madonna co-starred in the movie *Desperately Seeking Susan.* The movie featured Madonna's song *Into the Groove.*

Madonna (right) in Desperately Seeking Susan

> **"** I have the same goal I've had ever since I was a girl. I want to rule the world. **"**
>
> Madonna

Madonna is the best-selling female artist of all time. Here, she performs on stage in 2005.

MICHAEL JACKSON

- 13 Number 1 singles
- 9 Number 1 hits in the 1980s
- 750 million records sold

Michael Jackson's *Thriller* is the best-selling album ever. It sold over 100 million copies.

Michael Jackson with zombies in the Thriller video

> **I didn't choose to sing or dance. But that's my role and I want to do it better than anyone else.**
>
> Michael Jackson

The music video for the single *Thriller* was 14 minutes long. It had a horror movie storyline. The video changed pop music forever. From that point on, the video was just as important as the song!

CHAPTER 5

THE 1990s

In the 1990s, manufactured pop would steal the show!

Manufactured groups were created by record producers. The producers put together groups of young, good-looking performers. They gave the groups catchy songs to sing.

The plan was to create groups who would become enormously famous and earn millions.

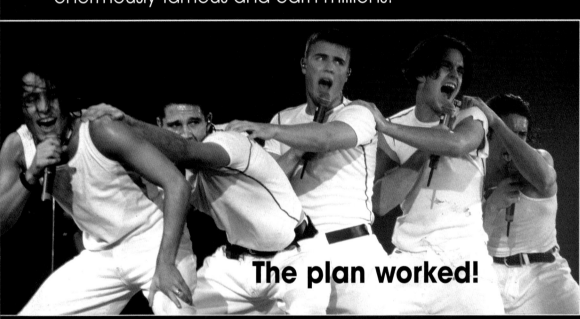

The plan worked!

Boy bands ruled manufactured pop.

Groups such as Backstreet Boys, Take That and *NSYNC delighted fans with their tuneful vocals and well-trained dance moves.

Baby Spice

Sporty Spice

Ginger Spice

Scary Spice

Posh Spice

The Spice Girls were a manufactured pop group.

Some people said the Spice Girls couldn't sing or dance. The group's fans did not agree!

The Spice Girls only recorded three albums. However, they have sold 55 million records worldwide.

1990s POP PROFILE
BRITNEY SPEARS

- 83 million records sold
- 800 awards won

Britney Spears was one of the biggest pop stars in the 1990s.

Britney's album *Baby One More Time* sold over 25 million copies worldwide. It was the best-selling album ever by a teenage solo artist.

" I want to be an artist that everyone can relate to, that's young, happy and fun. **"**

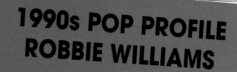

1990s POP PROFILE
ROBBIE WILLIAMS

- 17 million singles sold
- 55 million albums sold

Robbie Williams was a member of the manufactured boy band Take That. He left the band and went solo in 1995.

In 2006, Robbie set a Guinness World Record when he sold 1.6 million tickets for his world tour in one day.

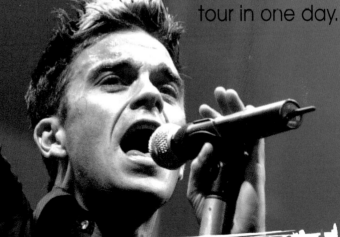

" I'm quite obviously not the world's most handsome man – I'm the second world's most handsome man! "

CHAPTER 6

THE 2000s

The 2000s belong to the pop divas!

Glamorous, talented singers such as Jennifer Lopez, Christina Aguilera and Beyoncé have all become huge superstars.

Their music is influenced by R&B and Hip-Hop music.

Christina Aguilera

Christina Aguilera has sold over 42 million albums worldwide. She has also won four Grammy awards.

In the 1980s, Kylie Minogue starred in the Australian soap opera, *Neighbours*. She moved to the UK to record the song *I Should Be So Lucky*. She became a huge pop star.

In the 2000s, Kylie is still wowing pop fans with new songs, glittering outfits, glossy videos and glamorous concerts.

Kylie has sold over 60 million records.

Kylie Minogue

In the 2000s technology has changed pop music.

Today, we download digital singles and albums from the Internet. We listen to them on computers, mobile phones and MP3 players.

Reality TV shows are creating pop stars. Singers perform on live TV shows. Then millions of viewers vote for their favourite artists by text or phone.

Shows such as *Pop Idol, American Idol* and *The X Factor* have produced pop stars such as Will Young, Kelly Clarkson and Leona Lewis.

Leona Lewis won the British TV show *The X Factor* in 2006.

Leona's first single, *A Moment Like This,* broke a world record. It was downloaded over 50,000 times within 30 minutes of being released.

NEED TO KNOW WORDS

blues A style of sad-sounding music. It came from the songs sung by black American slaves and farm workers.

chorus The part of a song repeated after each verse.

country music A simple style of music played on banjos, violins and guitars. It is often thought of as "cowboy music".

diva This word was once used to describe popular, female opera singers. Today, it is often used to describe all famous female singers.

funk music A style of popular dance music. It has strong, rhythmic backing on bass guitar and drums.

Grammy awards Music awards given each year by the "American National Academy of Recording Arts and Sciences".

Hip-Hop A style of music with rap lyrics over electronic music.

influence When one thing shapes or has an effect on something else.

Latin music A style of rhythmic dance music from South and Central America, Spain and Portugal.

professional Someone who is paid to do something.

R&B (Rhythm and Blues) Rhythm and blues is a combination of blues, soul, gospel and jazz music. It was invented by black musicians in the 1940s. R&B in the 2000s, features dance, disco, Hip-Hop and soul music.

rebellious Disobeying or disagreeing with authority.

record producer A person who works with music artists in a recording studio to help them create their music.

soul music A music style that combined the gospel music heard in black American churches with rhythm and blues.

verse Groups of lines that, with a chorus, form the words of a song.

vision The ability to plan the future with imagination or wisdom.

30

MORE POP FACTS

- In 2002, Elvis made a comeback – even though he died in 1977. He scored a Number 1 hit when his song *A Little Less Conversation* was remixed and re-released.

- The Beatles had more Number 1 hits than any other band. They could have had more. However, they were often competing with their own song that was already at Number 1.

ABBA

- ABBA have sold over 400 million records worldwide. They still sell up to 4 million albums every year – even though they split up in 1982.

POP MUSIC ONLINE

Websites

http://www.billboard.com/
A music magazine for pop fans

http://www.mtv.com/
A website featuring MTV news, shows and music videos

http://www.bbc.co.uk/music/
An information website about music from around the world

INDEX